CARROT

Christopher Trotter

Photography by Caroline Trotter

*For my mother
who gave me the love of cooking*

© Christopher Trotter 2016

Published by Christopher Trotter.

A CIP catalogue record for this book is available from the British Library.

ISBN 978-0-9926830-4-7

Produced by Print & Design, University of St Andrews
Website: www.st-andrews.ac.uk/printanddesign

Printed by Latimer Trend & Company Limited

Distributed by Christopher Trotter
Tel: 07739049639

CONTENTS

INTRODUCTION

Why choose carrots? Well this is my fourth book on vegetables and following on from the predominantly purple beetroot and green courgette and kale, the orange colour was immediately appealing! Carrots are so versatile and can be eaten both raw and cooked; their natural sweetness lends them to being a sugar substitute. They were used as a sweetener in the war in cakes etc. and surely carrot cake must be one of the most well known of popular cakes. (There is no recipe here as there must be hundreds available, indeed, there is one in one of my previous books!) But there is a carrot tart.

As a child I remember the problems my mother had growing carrots, because of the notorious carrot fly, she found it hard but not impossible. She used to grow them combined with certain flowers or perhaps garlic, choosing out of the way parts of the garden to hide from these irritating insects. But she must had some success as I do have memories of pulling carrots straight from the ground and giving them a cursory wipe and eating them, there and then, and enjoying the aromatic fresh sweet but earthy smell giving way to that wonderful crunch.

Cultivated carrots originated in the Middle East, and their use and cultivation slowly spread around the Mediterranean. They were red, white and yellow and the orange variety only began in the sixteenth century, possibly as a symbol of support to William of Orange during the Dutch wars of independence from the Spanish. From there they came over to England and have developed ever since.

VARIETIES

There are many varieties which have been developed over the years, and although many are not available in the shops, it's worth having a go at growing your own; however this is not a guide to growing! But it's worth looking out for different varieties as some are more suitable with certain recipes than others, Salads in particular need colourful crisp varieties, dishes with a whole carrot can benefit perhaps from the small round varieties and these too are great in a child's school lunch box. Long ones are great for the dishes needing strips such as the parfait or lasagne. As stated before Carrots were developed in the Middle East from wild carrots which in themselves are woody and not really edible. Old British varieties include "Altringham" from the 1800's, very long and a deep red colour. "Long red Surrey" is another similar also with great flavour. Of the more modern varieties there is "purple haze" purple on the outside and orange in the middle, which I have used in some of the pictures. "Yellowstone" a sweet carrot and yellow in colour good for carrot cakes or the carrot tart and in dishes with lots of coloured carrots. A round one is "Paris Market" which should be harvested young. Riverford grow commercially "Artemis" "Narvonne" and "Nepal" to name a few but the favourite for flavour is the old fashioned "Autumn King". Red carrots are often called Pakistani carrots as the varieties grown there tend to be red, as they have been for hundreds of years, they can be found in Asian supermarkets.

SEASONS

Carrots in the UK are generally sown from January to May and harvested from June until November and then stored, covered, in the ground or are lifted and kept in cold store so we have "fresh" carrots year round. As with beetroot the way to know if they really are fresh is by buying them with their green fronds still attached.

NUTRITION

The different colours tend to dictate levels of different healthy properties, so this is a guide only. They contain lycopene a pigment which is associated with the reduced risk of Macular degeneration, an age related disease which leads to the causes of blindness in the elderly. It also helps prevent heart disease and a variety of cancers including prostate cancer. It also helps maintain healthy skin. Carrots are rich in beta carotene which helps vision and it was put out by the propaganda people in the Second World War that pilots were eating carrots which helped them see in the dark, thus keeping radar a secret for a few months longer! It is also said to slow down aging. Vitamin A helps the skin, protecting it from sun damage and helps to clean out the liver. The roughage also helps to keep the gut clear and healthy. Crunching on a raw carrot helps to keep teeth clean and healthy. They are also said to help reduce the likelihood of a stroke. Other nutrients include copper, manganese and phosphorus.

CARROT, MUTTON & BARLEY BROTH

A take on a classic Scotch broth. By using only carrots as the vegetable, the sweetness really sets off the richness of the mutton, and, let's be honest, Scotch broth traditionally would be made with mutton not lamb! A very economical dish, as you even use all the trimmings from the vegetables.

INGREDIENTS

2 necks of mutton just under a kilo
2 tblsp cold-pressed rapeseed oil
1 onion, peeled and chopped
1 stick celery, chopped
1 leek, chopped
Sprig fresh thyme
Bay leaf

1 tsp peppercorns
100g pearl barley, rinsed in
    cold water
500g carrots chopped
1 tsp Hebridean seaweed sea salt
Freshly ground black pepper
1 tblsp chopped fresh coriander

METHOD

1   Turn the oven to 220C, gas mark 7, and roast the mutton necks for about 20 minutes or until browned all over. Place in a large pot and just cover with cold water and bring to the boil.
2   Place the trimmings from the onions, carrots, leek and celery into the roasting pan and stir around to coat in the mutton fat and, roast in the oven for a further 10 minutes to colour also.
3   When the necks come to the boil, reduce heat to a simmer and skim off any froth. Add the roasted vegetable trimmings, the herbs and pepper corns and simmer for a couple of hours until the meat falls from the bones. Set aside to cool.
4   In another pot, sweat the chopped onion and leek in the oil for a few minutes and then add the celery, followed by the barley; stir to mix through.
5   Strain the stock from the necks onto the barley and bring to a simmer. Cook for 20 minutes.
6   Remove all the meat from the necks and cut into pieces and discard the bones and vegetable trimmings.
7   After the 20 minutes simmering, add the diced carrots and cook for another 10 minutes; stir in the reserved meat, check for seasoning and serve with chopped coriander.

9

HAKE IN CARPIONE

Carpione means simply soused or pickled, but vinegar is the thing. However, carrot and its natural sweetness cuts through the vinegar allowing the magnificent and underestimated hake to sing. One of my much admired chefs, Rowley Leigh, suggests this as a picnic dish.

INGREDIENTS

750g hake fillet
1 tsp smoked Hebridean sea salt
3 shallots
1 red chilli, seeded and finely chopped
150ml white wine vinegar
150ml olive oil
3 bay leaves
1 tsp black peppercorns
200g baby carrots or chantenay
200g spring onions

METHOD

1   Cut the hake into small 60g pieces, and season with the smoked salt.
2   Peel and thinly slice the shallots and place in a pan with the chilli, vinegar, oil, bay leaves and peppercorns. Bring to the boil and simmer very gently for 15 minutes, and then pour over the fish. Allow to cool, cover and refrigerate overnight.
3   Blanche and refresh the carrots and spring onions and place in a bowl. Carefully place the fish on top and add a spoonful or two of the marinade. Chill until ready to serve.

CHICKPEAS WITH CARROTS AND CHARD

A simple accompaniment for fish or lamb but a good dish on its own. You can use canned chickpeas to save time, but cooking them yourself with garlic adds great flavour!

INGREDIENTS

100g dried chickpeas soaked in water overnight
1 head of garlic
2 tblsp olive oil, plus more to dress
1 medium onion, finely chopped
Clove garlic, crushed, with a little sea salt
300g carrots, diced
Tin chopped tomatoes
1 tsp tomato puree
200g chard, stalks removed and finely shredded
1 tblsp chopped mint
Hebridean sea salt and ground black pepper

METHOD

1   Drain the chickpeas and put into a pan with the garlic head sliced in half through the middle; cover with water, bring to the boil and simmer gently for an hour or so until tender.
2   Drain, remove the garlic, season with salt and pepper and a little olive oil.
3   Heat 2 tblsp olive oil in a pan and gently sweat the chopped onion to soften, add the crushed garlic, chard stalks and carrots and continue to cook for 10 minutes.
4   Stir in the tinned tomatoes and the puree, and cook to thicken slightly.
5   Tear up the chard leaves into manageable pieces and stir into the mixture with the mint; check for seasoning and add some more olive oil.

ROAST CARROT WITH PINE NUTS AND GREEN DRESSING

This recipe needs a carrot of uniformity and colour. The sweet Nantes variety would be ideal, as simply cut lengthwise they present themselves beautifully, but any young carrot will do.

The dressing can be used with other sweet roast vegetables such as parsnips; a lovely summer lunch dish.

INGREDIENTS

6 Nantes carrots
2 tblsp cold-pressed rapeseed oil
Mixed, colourful salad leaves – rocket, baby chard and red lettuce
2 tblsp pine nuts, dry roasted

Dressing
1 ripe avocado
2 tblsp fresh coriander
Handful of basil leaves
Juice of a lime
1 tsp honey
120ml water
Hebridean sea salt; the smoked one goes well
Freshly ground black pepper

METHOD

1   Preheat the oven to 200C, gas mark 6.
2   Cut the carrots into even sizes; if Nantes, cut as in intro, and toss in the oil to coat, and sprinkle with a little salt. Roast for 20 minutes until the carrots still have a little "bite" but are browning at the edges.
3   Whizz the dressing ingredients in a blender to create a thick texture.
4   Mix the carrots with the leaves and sprinkle with the pine nuts, dot with blobs of the dressing.

CRUSHED ROAST CARROTS WITH CUMIN AND GOATS' CHEESE

A simple little mezze idea, in which case it's good with Lebanese breads or as a first course with toast or oat cakes; a small pestle and mortar is useful for crushing spices.

INGREDIENTS

750g carrots, cut in lengths evenly
½ tsp Hebridean Sea salt
4 tblsp cold-pressed rapeseed oil, plus extra for dressing
2 tsp cumin seeds, dry toasted and crushed
100g crumbly goats' cheese
2 tblsp sunflower seeds, dry toasted
1 tblsp chopped oregano

METHOD

1   Preheat the oven to 180C, gas mark 4.
2   Toss the carrots in the oil with a little salt and roast for about 50 minutes until soft and lightly browned.
3   Roughly mash them, seasoning with the roasted cumin and a little more salt if required.
4   Spread onto a plate or into a bowl and sprinkle with the crumbled goats' cheese, sunflower seeds and herbs.

ROAST YOUNG CARROTS, SMOKED VENISON AND CROWDIE

This is best with really fresh carrots from the garden; their natural sweetness does not need to be enhanced with sugar; instead, the fresh herbs and the strong smoked flavour of the venison with the rich creaminess of the Crowdie works perfectly. For my photograph, I actually had some colourful carrots so I sliced them on the angle, looks pretty!

Anja Baak, at Great Glen Foods, makes a lovely smoked wild venison, and Crowdie is a traditional Scottish curd cheese; the best comes from Jill and Callum Clark's organic Connage dairy

INGREDIENTS

1kg fresh young carrots, trimmed
50g butter
2 cloves garlic
Sprig thyme
Sprig rosemary

Pack of smoked venison (approx. 75g)
Hebridean sea salt
Freshly ground black pepper
Olive oil or cold-pressed rapeseed oil

METHOD

1   Place the butter in a frying pan, and as it foams up throw in the carrots, garlic, herbs and seasoning. Allow to colour, takes about 10 minutes, then cover, reduce the heat and cook gently for another 10 minutes.
2   Pull away from the heat and set aside for 15 minutes.
3   Remove the lid and shake the pan to coat the carrots in the juices. Brush off the herbs and garlic. Place the carrots on individual plates or a serving dish and dress with the smoked venison, and little spoonfuls of Crowdie.

ROAST CARROT, CORIANDER AND CHICKPEA SALAD

Picnic food which will satisfy the most conservative of tastes, as well as the more adventurous. You can replace the chickpeas with any tinned beans you like. This is ideal for the tiny round carrots simply cut into quarters.

INGREDIENTS

10 round carrots
Hebridean sea salt
2 tblsp virgin olive oil
400g tin of chickpeas
Good bunch of coriander, washed and chopped
1 tblsp sesame seeds, dry toasted
Juice of an orange
1 tsp poppy seeds

METHOD

1   Mix the carrots with a little olive oil and some Hebridean salt and roast for 30 minutes.
2   Once cooked, mix with the chickpeas, herbs and seeds.
3   Make a dressing with the orange juice and remaining olive oil, and dress the salad. Sprinkle with the poppy seeds.

Delicious warm, but also good cold.

MORROCAN CARROT SOUP

Carrot soup is a well-known British staple, so here is a spicy version.

INGREDIENTS

500g carrots grated
50g butter
1 onion peeled and grated or finely chopped
2 cloves garlic, crushed
½ tsp turmeric
½ tsp ginger
½ tsp cinnamon
½ tsp paprika
½ tsp cumin
1.25 litres stock
50g couscous
Juice of half a lemon
1 tbslp chopped flat parsley

METHOD

1   Soften the onion in the butter in a large pan, add the garlic and spices and cook gently for a few minutes.
2   Add the carrot and stock, bring to the boil, cover and cook gently for 10 minutes.
3   Stir in the couscous until simmering again and cook covered for a further 15 minutes.
4   Swirl in the lemon juice, check for seasoning, and serve with the parsley.

CARROT AND ORANGE SALAD

A simple but refreshing salad, ideal for a summer bbq. The juice for marinating the carrot is not all needed for the salad, so you can drink the rest!

INGREDIENTS

3 oranges
500g carrots
2 tblsp lemon juice
1 tsp ground cinnamon
1 tblsp caster sugar
1 tblsp orange flower water
Pinch Hebridean sea salt
1 tsp shredded mint leaves

METHOD

1   Peel and segment the oranges. Slice off the top and bottom of the oranges; using downwards and even strokes, slice the skin from the flesh. Remove any white pith, and then cut between the membranes to segment the oranges; set aside the segments. Squeeze out the juice from the remaining central core and discard with the skin.

2   Peel and cut the carrots into fine strips. You can use a mandolin to do this or cut the carrots into 2.5 cm batons and slice thinly to make 'matchsticks'.

3   Mix the orange juice with the lemon juice, cinnamon, flower water, sugar and a little salt. Then combine with the carrots, refrigerate for an hour or so.

4   When coming to serve the dish, place the orange segments on a plate, drain the carrots and sprinkle over the top. Pour over a little of the juice (drink the rest!) and dust with a little more cinnamon and shredded mint.

SPICED CARROTS

Another North African idea. This can be served cold but is best warm and goes well with lamb.

INGREDIENTS

½ tsp Hebridean sea salt
500g carrots cut into batons
½ tsp paprika
½ tsp cumin
2 tblsp chopped flat parsley
1 tblsp lemon juice
2 tblsp olive oil

METHOD

1   Cook the carrots in boiling salted water until just cooked; don't overdo it, as the carrots will cook a little longer as they sit. Drain and mix with all the other ingredients and a little more salt.
2   Leave for at least an hour and serve. If completely cold, you can warm them up briefly, with some oil.

CARROT HALVA

This is a pudding from Pakistan and is traditionally made with a translucent red carrot which is indigenous to the region. Red carrots are often referred to as "Pakistani" carrots.

For the picture, I sprinkled over some fresh blackcurrants, as much for colour as anything, but actually the sharp tang of the fruit really cut through the sweetness of the pud.

INGREDIENTS

675g red carrots
675ml milk
Pinch saffron
½ tsp ground cardamom
340g granulated sugar
100g sultanas
100g unsalted butter
1 tbslp toasted flaked almonds

METHOD

1   Peel and finely shred the carrots, a food processor does a great job.
2   Bring the milk to the boil and add the carrots, saffron and cardamom; return to a simmer, cover and cook over a very low heat, or in a low oven for an hour, stirring from time to time. Stirring is very important; it helps to break it down to a soft mixture.
3   20 minutes before the end stir in the sultanas.
4   Stir in the butter to melt, and then press into a bowl and chill.
5   To serve you can turn the pudding out and decorate with the almonds, or just scoop out spoonfuls.

CARROT CROQUETTES

A bit retro maybe, but nevertheless a delicious way to serve carrots and children love them!

The initial cooking in water, speeds the cooking up and allows the processing to achieve a smooth texture. You can of course add chopped herbs for a bit of colour.

INGREDIENTS

1 kg carrots cut in similar sized barrels
Hebridean sea salt
40g butter
2 eggs
5 tblsp grated Grana Padano
Pinch of nutmeg
Freshly ground black pepper
Fresh breadcrumbs
Dried breadcrumbs
500ml oil for deep fat frying

METHOD

1   Bring a pan of water to the boil and add a tsp Hebridean sea salt.
2   Throw in the carrots and cook for 15 minutes, drain and allow to cool slightly. Blitz in a food processor until quite smooth.
3   Heat the butter in a frying pan and cook this mixture for ten minutes; allow to cool for a few minutes and tip into a large bowl.
4   Mix in the grated Grana Padano and beat in the eggs; season with salt, pepper, and nutmeg, mix in enough fresh breadcrumbs to form a firm mixture. Shape into small croquettes and chill.
5   Roll in the dried breadcrumbs and deep fry until crisp and golden.

CHICKEN STOCK

Carrots play a very important part in flavouring stocks. They add a rich sweetness and along with onions and celery are an essential ingredient. These three will go into any stock, be it for meat, fish or vegetable. So just to give a taste, here is a recipe for the easiest of all, a chicken stock. Please start with a good whole chicken, by that I mean at the very least free range or organic. The flavour is so much better, not to mention the nutritional value and the carcass... well that gives the stock its flavour!

INGREDIENTS

1 chicken carcass
2 carrots, including trimmings
    and tops
1 medium onion, studded with
    4 cloves
2 sticks celery

1 tsp black peppercorns
Bay leaf
Parsley stalks, sprig thyme and
    rosemary
1 clove garlic crushed
Water

METHOD

1   Once you have eaten and enjoyed your chicken, roughly chop up the carcass; don't forget the leg and wing bones, and roast in a hot oven until lightly brown; this gives the stock its colour.
2   Place the carcass in a large pot, cover with cold water and bring to the boil.
3   Roughly chop the vegetables, and roast in the tin used for the carcass, stirring them in the juices left by the carcass, to lightly colour.
4   When the carcass comes to the boil, turn the heat down to a gentle simmer and skim off any impurities. Add the vegetables, herbs, garlic and peppercorns, simmer gently for an hour. Allow to cool and strain.

The stock will keep in the fridge for 4 or so days; use for soups, risotti and sauces.

MIREPOIX
(with whole cooked salmon)

It may seem odd that I give a recipe for this but, as with the stock above, it is a culinary essential. Mirepoix can be used for braising meats in a pot roast and for adding flavour to poaching fish; so, as I used chicken for the stock above, I will use fish for the mirepoix.

A mirepoix is simply cut onions, carrots and celery. It is always worth cutting them evenly so they look the same and of course they will cook at the same time; for different foods you can add other flavours such as leek or shallots.

Poached whole salmon

Ideally, a fish kettle is the item required but often it's not very big; If you do have one, it allows you to cook the fish and lift it out of the water easily. However, I find that a roasting tray with a small cooling rack in the base is enough and you can lift the fish out easily. It just needs covering in foil to cook, but otherwise the following recipe is fine.

INGREDIENTS

One whole salmon
    approx 2-2.25 kg
1 onion peeled and sliced
2 carrots thinly sliced
Stick celery, sliced

Fennel fronds (optional)
A few peppercorns
2 bay leaves
4 tblsp white wine vinegar
1 tsp Hebridean seaweed sea salt

METHOD

1   Place the salmon on the trivet for the fish kettle and put it into the kettle.
2   Add the ingredients, then cover with cold water and bring to the boil over a medium heat.
3   Once boiling, switch off the heat and leave the fish to cool. You can either leave it to cool completely, or just for an hour or so and serve it warm. Either way, lift it out and scrape off the skin using a sharp knife; it will come away easily. Dress on a long dish.

CARROT IN SWEET VINEGAR

A refreshing Japanese side dish. Good as an accompaniment with dishes such as Teriyaki, this comes from Emi Kazuko's book Japanese Cooking which she has signed for me, but as it is in Japanese script I have no idea what she has said!

INGREDIENTS

2 large carrots peeled
1 tsp Hebridean sea salt
75ml rice vinegar
30ml shoyu
45ml mirin
2 tblsp sesame seeds, dry roasted

METHOD

1   Cut the carrots into thin strips as in the carrot and orange salad (page 25).
2   Mix with the salt and leave for 20 minutes, then rinse thoroughly and drain.
3   Mix together the marinade ingredients and mix through the carrot, leave for 3 hours.
4   When ready to serve, place the carrots in the serving bowl, chop the seeds, and sprinkle over.

CARROT PARFAIT

This is one to play with! I loved the idea of a mould with thin carrot strips and something inside. This is a carrot book so it's carrots all the way, but you could line this mix with smoked salmon or put a smoked salmon mouse inside the carrot! Experiment!

INGREDIENTS

4 large carrots
2 tsp butter
2 shallots, finely chopped
Sprig thyme and marjoram
200ml milk

100ml cream
2 eggs
Hebridean sea salt
Freshly ground black pepper

METHOD

1   Using a peeler, peel the carrots as far as you can, getting nice even thin strips.
2   Blanche these in boiling, salted water for a minute and refresh in cold water, drain and dry on kitchen towel.
3   Dice the remaining bits of carrot and make up to approx. 225g with extra carrots.
4   Take a pan and sweat the shallots in the butter, stir in the carrots and mix in, add the herbs, rubbing them as you drop them in. Cook for a few minutes to get a real heat going without burning.
5   Add a splash of boiling water, cover and leave to steam gently for a few minutes.
6   Remove the lid and continue to cook over a low heat until the carrots are soft and the mixture quite dry.
7   Blitz in a food processor, scraping down the sides a few times and then add the milk and really process 'til smooth. Add the cream and eggs, mix thoroughly, then pour into a jug and season. You can add some chopped fresh herbs, if you like.
8   Turn the oven to 180C, gas mark 4.
9   Butter some dariole dishes or ramekins and then line them with the blanched carrot strips, using the long ones to go from side to side and then the shorter ones to fill in the gaps.
10 Fill with the mixture, gently bending any overhanging carrot strips back over the mousse. Cook in a bain marie for about 40 minutes until just set, chill.
11 Finally, dip the dariole bases in hot water for a few minutes and shake out on to plates. Serve with salad and toast.

CARROT BAKE

A very simple dish which can be an accompaniment to meat or as a dish on its own, served with greens as in this picture. The cheese gives it a good texture. I use St Andrews Farmhouse cheese, made by the wonderful Jane Stewart.

INGREDIENTS

225g carrots, grated
½ tsp Hebridean sea salt
50ml vegetable stock
Medium onion finely chopped (red gives a nice pink fleck)
200g cheddar cheese, grated
2 eggs, lightly beaten
1 tsp vegetable oil
Freshly ground black pepper
2 tsp chopped fresh coriander

METHOD

1   Preheat oven to 180C, gas mark 4.
2   Mix the salt and grated carrot together and place in a pan over a low heat, gently sweat to dry out.
3   Pour in the vegetable stock and again cook gently until it dries out, about 5 minutes, then set aside.
4   In a frying pan, sweat the onion in the oil until soft but not coloured.
5   Mix into the carrots and add the coriander, grated cheese and eggs. Season and spread into a baking dish; smooth off and bake for 15 minutes

CARROT FRITTERS

These are delicious if deep fried. They make great snacks and go well with Trotter's hot pepper jelly, and a glass or two of beer!

INGREDIENTS

1 tsp ground cumin
1 tsp ground coriander
¼ tsp turmeric
100g wholemeal flour
50g plain flour
1 tsp Hebridean sea salt
125ml cider
1 egg, lightly beaten
200g carrots, grated
1 bunch spring onions, finely chopped
1 tblsp chopped mint
500ml oil for deep fat frying

METHOD

1   Mix the spices with the flours and then make a batter with the cider and egg.
2   Squeeze out any excess moisture from the grated carrot and mix into the batter with the spring onions and mint. Season with Hebridean salt; the sea weed one works well.
3   Form blobs of mixture on a pudding spoon and drop into hot oil until brown all over; takes about 5 minutes.

LEBANESE COLESLAW

I discovered sumac a few years ago, travelling in the Middle East, and use it with care. I am used to seasoning with lemons; it's hard to get away from that form of seasoning tradition, but if you want that tang, without too much moisture, sumac's good to use, and of course authentic.

INGREDIENTS

2 shallots, finely sliced
1 tblsp balsamic vinegar
2 tsp soft brown sugar
2 tblsp sultanas
½ green cabbage, core removed, and finely shredded
½ celeriac, peeled and finely sliced into matchsticks
2 large carrots grated
3 tblsp extra virgin olive oil
Zest and juice of 2 oranges
2 tsp sumac
½ tsp Hebridean sea salt
Freshly ground black pepper
1 tblsp chopped coriander
2 tblsp pine nuts, toasted
Seeds from a pomegranate

METHOD

1   Place the shallots in a bowl with the vinegar and sugar, leave for 30 minutes.
2   Pour boiling water on to the sultanas and leave them similarly.
3   Mix the cabbage, celeriac and carrot with the shallot mixture.
4   Make a dressing with the oil, juice, zest and sumac.
5   Drain the sultanas and mix all together in a bowl, and season.

Dress with the toasted pine nuts and pomegranate seeds and sprinkle with the chopped coriander.

SWEET AND SOUR CARROTS

A simple way of cooking carrots as an accompaniment to a roast such as chicken or lamb. Good for young carrots where you can cook them whole, the round carrots work especially well for this.

INGREDIENTS

500g young whole carrots
50g butter
50g sugar
100ml white wine vinegar
Sprig thyme
Sprig rosemary
Clove garlic crushed
Hebridean seaweed sea salt
Freshly ground black pepper

METHOD

1   Colour the carrots with butter in a pan, add the sugar and caramelise lightly.
2   Add the vinegar and reduce by a half; just cover with water and add the thyme, rosemary and garlic and cook gently until just tender.
3   Remove the carrots and set aside to keep warm, discard the thyme rosemary and garlic.
4   Reduce the liquid to a glaze and return the carrots.

CARROT MASH

Almost too simple to put in as a recipe! But not quite... it's the drying that is important; once made, you can add your own seasonings: nutmeg, coriander or chopped fresh herbs, orange zest etc. Really good with game dishes.

INGREDIENTS

350g carrots
350g swede (orange turnip)
100ml double cream
Hebridean sea salt
Freshly ground black pepper

METHOD

1   Cut up the carrot and swede into even pieces, so they cook at the same time.
2   Place in a pan and cover with cold water, add a tsp of salt and bring to the boil, simmer gently until just cooked – about 30 minutes.
3   Drain and return the pan to the hob at a low temperature and shake from time to time to really dry out the vegetables, about 5 minutes.
4   Mash, or, for a smooth mixture, place in a food processor and whizz to a puree. Add the double cream and puree even smoother! Season.

CARROT SORBET

The only recipes I found for this used only carrot juice, and as fan of Michael Pollan I don't believe in juicing, preferring to use the whole vegetable, if at all possible. So I have experimented and came up with this refreshing, textured sorbet. If you don't have a sorbet machine, just freeze the mixture until nearly solid and ice crystals have formed, then place in a food processor and whizz, return to the freezer and it will freeze like a sorbet. You will need to leave it out of the freezer for a few minutes to soften before scooping.

INGREDIENTS

200g sugar
200ml water
300g fresh young carrots, peeled
Juice of a lemon
2 egg whites
50ml vodka (optional)

METHOD

1   Make a sugar syrup by simmering the water and sugar together for 5 minutes, cool.
2   Place the carrots in a food processor and blitz, scraping the sides down every so often until you have a smoothish mixture.
3   Pour in the syrup and lemon juice and process again until its gets really smooth.
4   Add the vodka, if using, and egg whites, process for another few minutes.
5   Place in the sorbet machine.

CARROT SOUFFLE

Once again, the stunning colour of carrots really makes this a wonderful dish and it's so simple to make. Soufflés are straightforward if you consider the science and make sure the variables are all as they should be. Experiment with different colours of carrots, and by all means change the spices to suit your taste.

INGREDIENTS

40g butter
40g plain flour, plus extra for
    preparing the soufflé dish
300ml full fat milk
Bay leaf, sprig thyme
Pinch allspice
¼ tsp Hebridean sea salt
1 egg white

Freshly ground black pepper
1 tsp mustard
160g grated raw carrot, squeezed
    to remove excess moisture
2 tsp grated hard cheddar. (I use
    St Andrews farmhouse.)
4 eggs

METHOD

1   Heat the milk in a pan with the herbs until just about boiling and then remove from heat; keep warm.
2   Separate the eggs, putting the whites plus the extra white in a large, clean, glass or stainless steel bowl. ,
3   Melt the butter in a pan over a low heat and stir in the flour, and cook gently for a few minutes without colouring. Strain the warm milk onto the butter/flour mixture and stir until it thickens. Add the seasonings, mustard, carrot, and egg yolks, beating in thoroughly.
4   Prepare a 1.2 litre soufflé dish by buttering thoroughly inside with a little softened butter using a pastry brush. Finish by brushing upwards from base to top; this helps the soufflé to rise evenly upward. Dust lightly with plain flour.
5   Turn the oven to 200C, gas mark 6.
6   Beat the egg whites with a pinch of salt, which helps to strengthen the albumen, until they form peaks, then fold a third into the carrot mixture. Next carefully pour the carrot mixture back into the egg white bowl, and gently fold in to combine. Pour into the prepared soufflé dish, sprinkle with the cheese and place in the hot oven; reduce the temperature to 180C, gas mark 4. Cook for up to 40 minutes but DON'T open the door for at least the first 15 or else the soufflé will fall! The soufflé should be brown and crisp on top, well-risen and slightly gooey in the middle.

CARROT AND LENTIL PATTIES — KOFTA

Another Middle-Eastern idea; they are quite loose and so need careful handling, but to add a Scottish touch I have rolled them in oatmeal which gives a nutty flavour and texture.

INGREDIENTS

3 large carrots grated
200g dried red lentils
1 tsp garam masala
1 red chilli, deseeded and finely chopped
2 tblsp chopped coriander or flat parsley
Hebridean sea salt
Medium ground oatmeal
Oil and butter for cooking

METHOD

1   Cook the carrot and lentils together in plenty of salted water for about 5 minutes, drain and allow to dry.
2   Blitz in a food processor to form a paste. Add the remaining ingredients and season with salt.
3   Cool the mixture and form into patties, chill.
4   Sprinkle some oatmeal on to a plate and season lightly with salt and pepper. Roll the patties in the oatmeal and fry in the butter and oil, until brown on both sides.

Serve with Trotter's hot pepper jelly and salad.

CARROT, COCONUT AND CORIANDER DIP

A refreshing dip with cruditees or crisps or as a spread.

INGREDIENTS

1 400ml can of coconut milk
2 tblsp cashew nuts
1 tsp peanut oil
2 cloves of garlic
2 cm piece ginger
1 red chilli seeded
6 large carrots, grated
1 tsp tomato puree
1 tblsp sunflower seeds, toasted
1 tblsp chopped fresh coriander
Juice of a lime
Hebridean sea salt

METHOD

1   Blitz the cashew nuts in a processor and pour in the oil to create a smooth paste.
2   In a pan, heat the coconut milk with the cashew paste, ginger, garlic and chilli, simmer for about 10 minutes.
2   Add the carrots and stir in the tomato puree and cook gently for another 10 minutes until the carrots are cooked through, add a little water if it seems dry.
3   Blend together with the toasted seeds and fresh coriander; season with the lime juice and Hebridean salt.

SPICY CARROT AND LENTIL CURRY

A simple vegetable curry with lots of different textures; serve on its own with rice and naan bread or along with a meat curry.

INGREDIENTS

1 tblsp cold-pressed
    rapeseed oil
1 onion, chopped
2 cm piece ginger, peeled
    and grated
4 cloves garlic crushed with salt
1 tsp chilli powder
1 tsp cumin
1 tsp ground coriander
2 tsp tomato puree

600ml vegetable stock
5 carrots cut into a large dice
1 or 2 lime leaves (optional)
200g red lentils rinsed
100g split, dried fava beans
200g frozen green peas
1 tblsp chopped coriander
Hebridean sea salt
Juice of a lime

METHOD

1   Take a large pot and heat the oil, add the onion and ginger and cook gently for a few minutes.
2   Stir in the spices and cook for another few minutes.
3   Stir in the carrots, lentils, dried fava beans, tomato puree and enough stock to cover. Simmer for 10 minutes until just cooked.
4   Add the peas and enough stock to cover again; simmer until hot through and then stir in the lime juice. You can either add the chopped coriander or sprinkle it on afterwards.

Like so many curries, this is often better the next day.

CARROT LASAGNE

This is a bit of fun really! Using real pasta for one layer and then thin strips of carrot for another; you can interchange of you like using all pasta or all carrot, as you please!

INGREDIENTS

30g butter
1 tblsp vegetable oil
1 leek trimmed and chopped
2 sticks celery, chopped
3 cloves garlic, crushed with a
    little salt
8 medium carrots

Handful of fresh basil, shredded
4 eggs lightly beaten
300ml double cream
Freshly ground black pepper
½ tsp Hebridean sea salt
5 sheets lasagne
200g grated goats' cheese

METHOD

1   Heat the oven to 180C, gas mark 4.
2   Peel the carrots into thin strips, just using the first few strips of each and then grate the remaining bits.
3   Heat the oil and butter in a pan and cook the leeks and celery together for a few minutes to soften; stir in the garlic and cook gently for a few more minutes.
4   Lower heat and add the grated carrots and cook gently, stirring occasionally, for another 5 or so minutes; stir in the basil.
5   Mix together the eggs, cream and seasoning.
6   Spread half the carrot mix on the base of an ovenable dish, and then cover with the lasagne sheets, pour on half the cream mix and half the goats' cheese.
7   Add the remaining grated carrot mix and cover with the strips of carrot; spread evenly with the remaining cream, and finish with the grated cheese.
8   Bake in the oven until brown and bubbling, about 50 minutes.

GRILLED ROE DEER FILLET, WITH CRUNCHY CARROT, TURNIP AND SESAME

This is inspired as much by Heston B's way with a steak tagliata as anything else, but the peppery flavours and crunchy textures make this a really quick but satisfying dish. It also works well with beef rump steak.

INGREDIENTS

2 roe deer fillets
Hebridean sea salt
Freshly ground black pepper
Cold-pressed rapeseed oil
3 large carrots cut in strips as per 'Carrot and Orange salad' (page 25)
2 white turnips thinly sliced as above

160g rocket
40g sesame seeds
Juice of a lemon
Splash sesame oil
50g Grana Padano cut into thin curls

METHOD

1 Make sure the roe deer fillets are up to room temperature and dried of any excess blood or moisture, and have all the other ingredients prepared.
2 Season and cook the fillets very quickly, searing the outsides in a very hot pan with just a dribble of oil. Cook as rare as you dare and set aside.
3 Mix the carrot and turnip and dress with the sesame oil and lemon juice. Place a little on the base of four plates.
4 Slice the fillets into reasonable pieces and place on top, then sprinkle with the carrot/turnip mix and the rocket. Finish with a few curls of cheese and a sprinkling of sesame seeds.

SAVOURY CARROT LAYER

I have the original Cranks recipe book to thank for this. The book is still on my shelves with the leaves sellotaped in! I wanted it to be in this picture but Caroline said it made it look "old fashioned" – but that's the point!

INGREDIENTS

450g carrots
Vegetable stock
25g butter
2 tblsp chopped parsley
1 tsp soy sauce
Hebridean sea salt
Freshly ground black pepper

For the topping:
25g butter
25g wholemeal flour
145ml whole milk
3 eggs lightly beaten
75g Anster cheese grated

METHOD

1 Turn the oven to 180C, gas mark 4.
2 Grate the carrots and cook them in a pan with 150ml of stock and salt for about 15 minutes.
3 Add the parsley and soy sauce and blend the mixture, adding more stock if necessary.
4 Check for seasoning and spread the mixture on the base of an ovenable dish.
5 Make a white sauce with the butter, flour and milk; away from the heat, beat in the eggs and then the cheese; check for seasoning.
6 Spread over the carrot mixture and bake for about 45 minutes.

CARROT TART

An unusual pudding, with which you can tease your guests as to the secret ingredient. Orange flower water does have a lovely fragrance, but don't worry if you can't find it; use grated orange and a little of its juice instead.

INGREDIENTS

225g short crust pastry
50g finely grated carrot
50g fresh breadcrumbs
2 egg yolks
1 egg white
150ml double cream
50g butter, melted and set aside
100ml brandy
1 tblsp orange flower water
2 tblsp caster sugar
Grated nutmeg

METHOD

1   Turn the oven to 180C, gas mark 4.
2   Line a 21cm tin with the pastry and bake blind.
3   Beat the eggs and cream together, fold in the carrot and bread crumbs.
4   Pour on the butter and brandy and stir through the flower water, sugar and nutmeg.
5   Pour into the blind baked pastry case and bake until risen slightly and has a golden crust, about 25 minutes.

BIOGRAPHIES

CAROLINE TROTTER is a freelance photographer and works across a wide variety of subjects. Weddings are her main area of work but she also does portraits, both human and animal – horses, dogs etc. Caroline covers events for associations such as Fife Chamber of Commerce and provides business portraits for websites and marketing purposes, and food photography for websites and restaurants. She also runs photography courses from home. She is a qualified member of the Master Photographers Association and the Society of Wedding and Portrait photographers.

www.carolinetrotter.co.uk

CHRISTOPHER TROTTER is Fife's Food Ambassador, an honorary title bestowed on him for his work promoting food from Fife. He is also a freelance chef, cookery writer and food commentator, appearing on programmes such as BBC Radio Scotland's *Kitchen Café* and *Kitchen Garden*. He is a committee member of The Guild Of Food Writers and is a sought after speaker at events and after dinner. As a consultant he has worked with agencies as diverse as Argyll and the Island's Enterprise and The National Trust for Scotland. Christopher also provides cookery classes and food tours and he is passionate about fresh produce in its season.

www.fifefoodambassador.co.uk

They have two children and two dogs and live in rural Fife.

ACKNOWLEDGEMENTS AND THANKS

This is book number four in my vegetable series and I have so enjoyed putting it together, and experimenting with different ideas, I have enjoyed exploring the eastern ideas as Carrots are from that region, so it seemed only right there should be a reflection of that in the book. I would like to thank the team at Waterstones in St Andrews for their continued support of the books, always friendly faces there!

The carrots in the photographs have come from Pillars of Hercules and Ardross farm shop so particular thanks to Bruce Bennett from the former and Claire from Ardross, and of course the pictures themselves which really make the books are taken by my lovely wife Caroline – Thank you. Once again my brother Graeme has edited it for me and Duncan Stewart at University of St Andrews Print & Design has put it all together – thank you both.

In the past I have acknowledged my "foodie heroes" but in the light of the task facing the country and the pressures on the NHS with the two main evils of today obesity and mental health. I firmly believe that cooking is the answer to these problems. Taking simple fresh produce, considering the seasons and involving children, in the daily and weekly cook can keep families, communities and friends together. The ultimate expression of being human is to cook and share a meal, Jamie Oliver is one person who has tirelessly campaigned for better food and for people to cook, a true food hero. I would also like to thank all those people who do care about where their food comes from and how they cook it.

HEBRIDEAN SEA SALT

Sea Salt Flakes harvested from the shores of the remote
Scottish Hebridean Isle of Lewis.

SIMPLY FROM THE SEA

Hebridean Sea Salt is Scotland's first gourmet salt producer. Nestled on
the banks of Loch Erisort, on the Isle of Lewis in the Outer Hebrides, we
harvest sea water from some of the most unspoilt coastline in the world.
The waters around the Hebrides are crystal clear and have been given
a grade A certification, which creates pure white crunchy sea salt flakes
that melt in the mouth.

PURE ORIGINAL SEA SALT

Our most popular variety, the Pure Original sea salt was the first to be
launched by the company in 2012. With over 60 naturally occurring
minerals such as essentials like Potassium, Zinc, Calcium & Magnesium
it is a wonderful alternative to table salts. It is best added to meals and
cooking by hand, 'a pinch' is just enough to enhance the natural flavours
of your food.

PEAT SMOKED SEA SALT

Delicately cold smoked with a mixture of oak and peat cut from the
surrounding moor, our peat smoked variety adds an extra depth
of flavour to any meal. Peat is very much a part of the Hebridean
landscape, the unmistakeable smell fills the air daily. Used as a rub for
meats, or on a simple salad, once you've started using our Peat Smoked
salt it will become a regular at every mealtime.

SEAWEED INFUSED SEA SALT

Our Pure Original sea salt and locally harvested seaweed make for the
perfect seasoning combination. With its rich and distinctive flavour
seaweed is packed full of essential nutrients. The people of the Hebrides
have been harvesting seaweed to supplement their diets for hundreds
of years. Use our Seaweed Infused sea salt to season fish, giving it an
added taste of the sea or in sushi or sauces. Seaweed also has a naturally
salty flavour, so this is a useful way to cut down on your salt in-take if
you need to.

AN AWARD WINNING RANGE

Hebridean Sea Salt is regularly awarded Great Taste stars at the annual Guild of Fine Food's 'Oscars' of the food world. We hope you will also find Hebridean Sea Salt a winning combination when teamed with your cooking.

NOTES

NOTES

NOTES